Contents

ETUDES

Edited by: Eric Wen

FRANZ WOHLFAHRT
Op. 45, Book 1

⊓ Herunterstrich.   ⊓ Tirez l'archet.   ⊓ Down bow.
V Hinaufstrich.   V Poussez l'archet.   V Up bow.

№ 1. Allegro moderato

f

Auch bei der zweiten, dritten und siebenten Etude benutze man die vor Etude I stehenden Stricharten.

Qu'on se serre a la seconde, troisième et septième Etude de la même manière de mener l'archet comme dans l'Etude Ire.

In the second, third and seventh Etude the same way of playing with the bow that has been indicated at the top of the first Etude is to be used.

№ 2. Allegro moderato

№ 3. Moderato

№ 4. Allegretto

№ 5. Moderato

№ 6. Moderato

6

№ 7. Allegro moderato

№ 8. Largo

№ 9. Allegretto

№ 10. Moderato

№ 11. Moderato

№ 12. Allegro

№ 13. Moderato

№ 14. Allegro non tanto

№ 15. Allegro

№ 16. Moderato

№ 17. Moderato assai

№ 18. Allegro

14

Bei den letzten 3 Takten behalte
man immer dieselbe Strichart bei.

Qu'on se serre toujours de la
même manière de mener l'archet
aux trois dernières mesures.

In the last three bars, the bowing
to be used in the same way of playing.

№ 19. Moderato

№ 20. Allegro

№ 21. Allegro

№ 22. Allegro

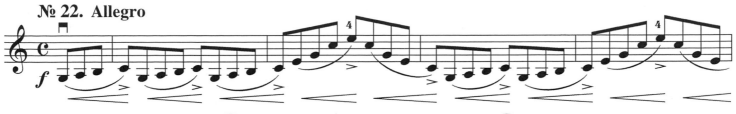

18

№ 23. Moderato

№ 24. Moderato assai

№ 25. Allegro

20

№ 26. Allegro

№ 27. Allegro

№ 28. Allegretto

№ 29. Moderato

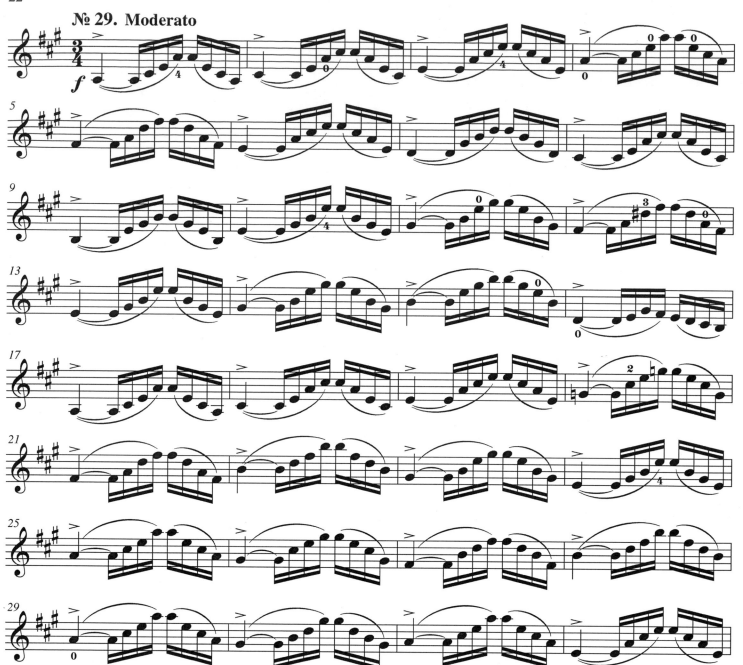

№ 30. Allegro

SELECTED VIOLIN SOLO AND CHAMBER MUSIC

Violin

Violin Etudes and Instruction

Wohlfahrt, Franz

S510005   Sixty Etudes for Violin, Op. 45, Bk. 1   HL 42303

2011 new issues--former Strad Magazine Editor-in-Chief, Eric Wen re-examines these classics with consideration for today's violinist. All editions newly engraved with handsome color covers and classic 9x12 ivory stock.

ed. Eric Wen

S510006   Sixty Etudes for Violin, Op. 45, Bk. 2   HL 42391

Violin Solo, unaccompanied

Adolphe, Bruce

X510011   Bitter, Sour, Salt Suite   HL 41866

Can be performed with or without narration, soloist can narrate.

Baker, David

S510001   Suite for Unaccompanied Violin   HL 40248

Recorded by Ruggerio Ricci on Laurel Records

Hartke, Stephen

X510012   Caoine   HL 41867

Name derived from the laments once sung by the professional wailing women of Ireland; also inspired by the folk fiddling tradition of the Shetland Islands.

Perkinson, Coleridge-Taylor

X510033   Blue/s Forms   HL 41886

Three-movement solo violin work fusing blues harmonic language with classical sonata form, recorded by Sanford Allen.

X510032   Louisiana Blues Strut: A Cakewalk   HL 41885

Recorded by Sanford Allen on Cedille Records "Coleridge-Taylor Perkinson: A Celebration"

Violin Solo with Keyboard

Baker, David

X511007   Blues (Deliver My Soul)   HL 41894

Recorded by Anne Akiko Meyers and Andre Michel-Schub, BMG Records..

S511005   Ethnic Variations on a Theme of Paganini   HL 40254

Commissioned By Ruggerio Ricci.

Cooman, Carson

X511035   Sonata for Violin and Organ   HL 41918

Crockett, Donald

X511039   Wet Ink for Violin and Piano   HL 42418

Violin and piano version of nonet by the same title, dedicated to Steven Stucky for his 60th birthday.

Dancla, Charles

S511010   Six Airs Varies for Violin and Piano, Op. 89   HL 42368

2011 new issues--former Strad Magazine Editor-in-Chief, Eric Wen re-examines these classics with consideration for today's violinist. All editions newly engraved with handsome color covers and classic 9x12 ivory stock.

ed. Eric Wen

Sevcik, Otakar

S511012   Sevcik Op. 16 Wieniawski Scherzo-Tarantelle with Analytical Exercises   HL 42327

Combines urtext quality solo material with exercises based on renowned 20th-Century violin pedagogue, Otakar Sevcik's, work.

ed. Stephen Shipps

S511014   Sevcik Op. 17 Wieniawski Concerto Op. 22 in D Minor with Analytical Exercises   HL TBDS511014

ed. Endre Granat

S511013   Sevcik Op. 19 Tchaikovsky Concerto Op. 35 in D Major with Analytical Exercises   HL TBDS511013

ed. Stephen Shipps

S511011   Sevcik Op. 21 Mendelssohn Violin Concerto in e minor with Analytical Exercises   HL 42326

ed. Endre Granat

Smith, John Stafford

S511015   The Star-Spangled Banner (Arranged for Violin and Piano by Jascha Heifetz)   HL 42616

Along with new engraving for his celebrated transcription, a photo from master violinist Jascha Heifetz's historical collection and a facsimile of the original autograph score adorn this commemorative 9x12 edition.

Stock, David

X511020   Santa Fe Salsa   HL 41905

For Andres Cardenes

Walker, George

X511038   Concerto for Violin and Orchestra (Piano reduction)   HL 42310

Dedicated to Violinist and Composer Gregory T.S. Walker. Recorded by Gregory Walker, violin and Sinfonia Varsovia, Ian Hobson Conductor, on Albany Records.

Walker, Gwyneth

X511015   Fantasy Etudes   HL 41900

Suite of short pieces which can be enjoyed by performers of all ages.

Violin Duo

Hartke, Stephen

X512001   Oh Them Rats Is Mean in My Kitchen   HL 41921

Scherzo-fantasy in homage to early blues, transforming its characteristic wailing and energetic speech-song into the seemingly incongruous medium of the violin duo

X512003   Two Shetland Bridal Tunes   HL 41923

Two arrangements of traditional Shetland Island fiddle tunes encompassing a processional and recessional, for any festive event or occasion.

Trios, mixed

Violin

Hartke, Stephen

X632711   The Horse with the Lavender Eye for Violin, Clarinet and Piano   HL 42074

Four movement tableau of vivid musical images bound together with skillfully crafted 'off-balance' motifs

---

Questions/ comments? Write to: info@laurenkeisermusic.com

LAUREN KEISER LK MUSIC PUBLISHING   KEISER CLASSICAL